ANCIENT ROME

Troll Associates

ANCIENT ROME

by Keith Brandt
Illustrated by Hal Frenck

Troll Associates

Library of Congress Cataloging in Publication Data

Brandt, Keith, (date)
    Ancient Rome.

    Summary: Briefly traces the development of the Roman
Empire, through which the city of Rome dominated the
western world for over five hundred years.
    1. Rome—Juvenile literature. [1. Rome. 2. Civili-
zation, Ancient] I. Frenck, Hal, ill. II. Title.
DG77.B726   1985   937   84-2684
ISBN 0-8167-0298-5 (lib. bdg.)
ISBN 0-8167-0299-3 (pbk.)

Copyright © 1985 by Troll Associates, Mahwah, New Jersey
All rights reserved. No part of this book may be used
or reproduced in any manner whatsoever without written
permission from the publisher.
Printed in the United States of America

10 9 8 7 6 5 4 3 2 1

Do you hear the busy sounds around us? We're in Rome—one of the world's most famous cities. Today it's the capital of Italy, but once it was the capital of the Western world.

Armies marched out of this city to keep the peace in faraway lands. Traders entered the city on horses and donkeys loaded with ivory, silk, and spices from Asia. Emperors built great palaces filled with riches.

There were royal zoos, too. They were filled with strange wild animals the Romans had never seen before—animals brought by ship from Africa: hump-backed camels, fierce lions, and tall giraffes.

All this happened more than 2,000 years ago. But even then, Rome was very old. There is an ancient story about how the city of Rome began—it's the legend of Romulus and Remus.

There were only a few farming families living on the flat land near the river then. The hills were full of deer and wolves. Twin baby boys came floating down the river in a basket. They were orphans—all alone and starving. A mother wolf found them and took them to her den in the hills, where she raised them as her cubs. The boys were named Romulus and Remus.

When Romulus grew up, he became a leader of the tribes of shepherds and farmers who lived in the area. Romulus and his

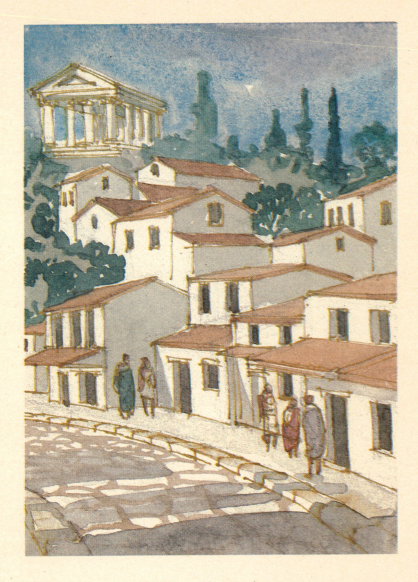

followers started a village that grew into one of the greatest cities in the world. That city is Rome, named after Romulus.

For a long time, Rome was a farm community. The town was surrounded by orchards of olive trees and fields of barley and grapevines.

At sunrise, the farmers left the town and went out to work their land. At sundown, they returned to the safety of home inside the city walls. Most activities centered around a warm and loving family life. The father was a strong figure whose rules were obeyed by the rest of the family.

The Romans believed in following rules. Hard work, duty, and courage were important to them. They made fair laws and obeyed them. They were good businessmen, too, because Roman law upheld *contracts*.

A contract is an agreement between businessmen that they will carry out their part of a bargain. Before Roman law was written, contracts could easily be broken. But under Roman law, a contract became a promise that would be kept.

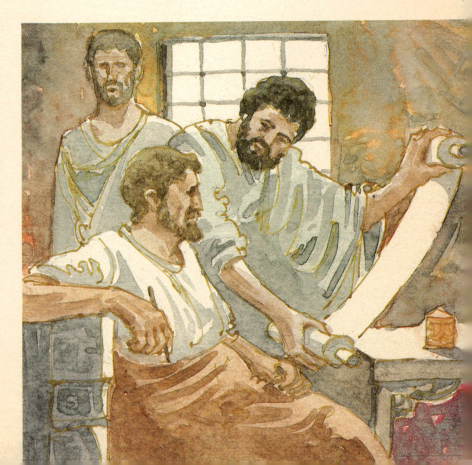

Good laws also gave Rome a well-organized government. In earliest times, Rome was ruled by kings who were sometimes cruel or unfair. In 509 B.C. , the Romans overthrew their king and organized a republic. They established a constitution that guaranteed rights to citizens.

Senators and government officials were elected to represent the people of Rome. Many modern ideas about government came from Rome. Some of our modern laws are Roman, too, like the idea that a person is innocent until proven guilty.

The Romans realized the importance of building good roads. The most famous Roman road is called the *Appian Way*. It leads from Rome all the way to the southern tip of Italy. The Appian Way was so well built that it's still in use today. Many roads like this helped Rome grow rich and strong. Traders and farmers used them to transport goods for sale.

Most of the roads in ancient Rome were built by the army. The courage and loyalty of the Roman soldiers made the army almost unbeatable. As Rome grew, more and more cities were conquered and ruled by Roman law.

While Rome was growing powerful, most of the land that is now Europe was still wilderness. The Romans thought the simple tribes of people living in Spain, France, and Germany were uncivilized. They called them *barbarians*, which meant "foreigners."

Roman generals brought in armies to take over the land and teach the people Roman ways. Roman roads and Roman law were laid down all across the land, as far north as present-day England. Roman governors ruled the barbarians. Many Roman cities sprang up, which copied the customs, the buildings, and even the plumbing of Rome.

Towns that had a single public well before Roman rule now had city-wide water systems. The Romans used underground

tunnels and pipelines on raised stone arches to carry water to the city. These water-bridges were called *aqueducts*, which means "water carriers." Some ancient Roman aqueducts are still in use today.

Most Roman towns had a community center where people could meet to bathe and swim. The city of Bath, in England, is named after the public baths and swimming pools the Romans built there long ago.

The general who led the victory over
England was Julius Caesar. Caesar was a
genius at waging war. Besides the victory

over England, Caesar led the Roman armies to victory in France, or Gaul, as France was called then. When Julius Caesar returned to Rome in 49 B.C., the people gave him a hero's welcome.

Rome was stronger and richer than ever. And Caesar soon became the leader of Rome. Rome needed a wise leader because the city had many problems. The slums were full of overcrowded apartment buildings and starving beggars. A huge gap existed between the lives of the rich and poor people.

Power belonged to the rich, who had special privileges. Often the poor went hungry or ate a simple meal of bread and onions, while the rich feasted at lavish banquets. Dressed in their gowns and jewels, women sat in chairs and men lay on couches. They drank fine wines and ate their fill of roasts, highly seasoned foods, and fresh fruit.

Wealthy families lived in big brick houses with sloping red tile roofs. Each house was built in the shape of a rectangle or square, with an open patio in the middle. A large entry room, called the *atrium*, had an opening in the roof to let the sun in. Parents, grandparents, children, and many servants all lived in these large houses.

One of the members of the household was likely to be a well-educated Greek slave, who served as a teacher for the family's children. For even though the Romans had conquered the Greeks in war, they admired the art and wisdom of Greece. Many of Rome's best artists and teachers were Greek. And most Roman statues and buildings were inspired by those of the Greeks.

Roman temples were much like the ones Greeks built to honor their gods. In fact, the Romans worshiped many of the Greek gods as their own and gave them Roman names. Even the Roman alphabet is a simplified form of the Greek alphabet—just as ours is a modern form of the Roman alphabet.

The Romans also adopted the old Greek idea of the town square as a public meeting place. In Rome this town center was called the *Forum*. Surrounded by courthouses, temples, and stores, it was a gathering place for lawyers and politicians, shoppers and worshipers. The Forum was a place to meet people, to trade news, and to gossip.

By the time of Julius Caesar, the original Forum was so crowded that he ordered another one built. Near the old Forum stood the Senate House, where Julius Caesar was murdered by jealous friends.

In his five short years as ruler of Rome, Caesar had accomplished a great deal. He had made the government more honest and set up a fair system of taxation. New construction had improved the slums, and

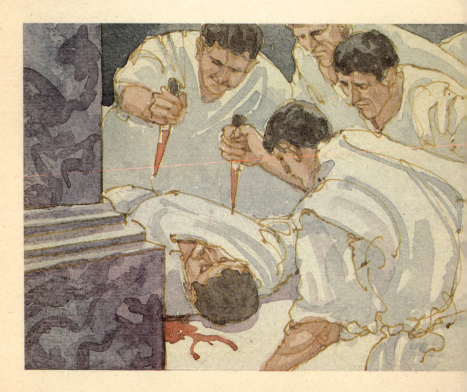

more people held jobs. Overcrowding had been cut down by moving people to settlements outside Rome.

Caesar had become so popular with the people of Rome that many had wanted to crown him and call him emperor. But others, who were jealous of him, murdered him in the Senate House on the Ides of March, 44 B.C.

The people who killed Caesar did not want a king. They feared Caesar's great power. But the next leader of Rome became an emperor anyway. After Caesar died, Rome was filled with fighting for years. The man who finally gained control of Rome was a relative of Caesar's named Octavian. Octavian took the royal name of *Augustus*, which means "Imperial Majesty."

Augustus was the first of many Roman emperors. He ruled the Roman Empire for forty years, bringing peace and progress. The great construction projects started by Caesar were continued. New temples, racetracks, sports stadiums, museums, and libraries were added to the city. So much was done that Augustus boasted, "I found Rome a city of bricks and left it a city of marble."

But the real secret of Rome's great structures was the strong concrete used to build them. Although a simple type of concrete was known back in Greek times, the Romans perfected its use. A good example is the Colosseum.

The Colosseum is a huge Roman sports stadium built of concrete. It was originally

covered with a decorative facing of marble. The marble was stolen hundreds of years ago, but the concrete shell is still standing. This famous arena is well known for the battles between lions and gladiators that were staged there. Other Roman entertainments were held in the Colosseum until the very end of the Roman Empire.

For over five hundred years, Rome was the greatest city of the Western world. But tribes of barbarians from the north finally overthrew Roman rule. Still, there are Roman ruins in many of Europe's great cities today. And the languages of France, Spain, and Portugal all grew out of Latin, the ancient Roman language. Europe is made up of many great countries now, but none will forget that Rome was once their teacher.